Summer
ROSES

RUBAB KHATRA

NewDelhi • London

BLUEROSE PUBLISHERS
India | U.K.

Copyright © Rubab Khatra 2024

All rights reserved by author. No part of this publication may be reproduced, stored in a retrieval system or transmitted in any form or by any means, electronic, mechanical, photocopying, recording or otherwise, without the prior permission of the author. Although every precaution has been taken to verify the accuracy of the information contained herein, the publisher assumes no responsibility for any errors or omissions. No liability is assumed for damages that may result from the use of information contained within.

BlueRose Publishers takes no responsibility for any damages, losses, or liabilities that may arise from the use or misuse of the information, products, or services provided in this publication.

For permissions requests or inquiries regarding this publication, please contact:

BLUEROSE PUBLISHERS
www.BlueRoseONE.com
info@bluerosepublishers.com
+91 8882 898 898
+4407342408967

ISBN: 978-93-5989-644-1

Cover design: Shivam
Typesetting: Namrata Saini

First Edition: October 2024

To my chosen family

Author's Note

Ironically I wrote this book with no intention of publishing it. However, I simply could not do with the snippets of my mind resting in a forgotten folder in my laptop when all I ever wanted was to have a voice which would remain eternal and tangible. Each poem is a snapshot offering a glimpse into the evolving moment which we hope to bottle up to either forevermore preserve or throw in the ocean to never find it again. This book is a deep personalised insight into the difficulties and confusion of transitioning into adulthood particularly the experiences, loses and ideals which unite and divide us. Through my journey writing this book I realised the importance of finding a connection and I hope this book is a friend to all in need of one because it was for me. You have my heart and soul...

Foreword

Dear Reader,

I hope you learn the best from my worst. How much can we do to make up for our lives? How much better can we expect ourselves to get until we are good enough? I've spent enough sleepless nights asking myself this question and now pass on the hysteria to you. We dig ourselves deeper and deeper, only to realize at the end that we could simply climb out. The answer to all my existential crises is ironically, the problem: We don't have enough time. We may make art of our misery and pain, but all we do is feel and step forward. I am not sure of a lot of things, but I do know that in the end, it's all going to be alright, and we would look back at the lost moments with nothing but regret. Be who you wanted to be as a child—the role model you wanted to become. Don't let your life be defined by trivial goals; instead, strive to be better than you were yesterday.

Contents

Be Who They Want You To Be But Don't Lose Yourself	1
You Don't Belong Here	3
Amalgamate	4
The Anarchist	5
The Home I Never Asked For	6
Red Phosphorous	8
One Last Drink First	9
Promise To Call When Free	11
The Ringleader	12
Give In	14
Fallen	15
Drink Me	17
Infringed	18
Me, Myself And I	19
Woman	21
Moonlight Swims	24
Tomorrow Was Worse	25
Ripple Drip	26
Lycanthropy	27
Battlegrounds	28
Blueprint	29
Why Does Pain Have To Have Purpose?	30

The Half-Broken Heart Necklace	31
You Have 0 Messages	33
The Child Born With A Broken Heart	36
The Mahogany Shelf With Bluebirds And Cherries	37
Make Mistakes But Don't Repeat Them	39
Dealer	40
Pride	41
Puppet	42
Break Me Or I Will Break You	44
Monday	46
They Call Me Cruel	47
Will You Be There For The Bedtime Story	48
Run	50
The Door Is Wide Open	52
Ice Sliding Down My Back	53
Alone And Lonely	54
The Girl With The Sun Tattoo	56
Participation Trophy	58
Smile For The Camera	59
Predictable	61
Captive	62
Void	64
Name	65
Bedside Tea	66
Bitten Back Words	67

Maps	68
The Better Whole But I Gave You My Half	70
Blackthorn Flowers	72
Letter	73
Come Back Nanu, "I Owe You"	74

Be who they want you to be but don't lose yourself

Horns grow hollow once the beast dies,
Just as the soul escapes through the windows of their eyes.
The vessels once pulsing with blood disappear,
Blend into the tissue of the interior,
Leaving no cue to mark their existence.
An orphic desinence
Much like mine;
For I was much less than an insordescent revenant,
Rose out of my pauper's grave,
Much like beauty and beast's rose,
Made of corroding metal,
A heterophemized symbol,
Thorns larger than the petals,
Gagged under the poundage of the medals,
Empty gold over pulse,
Suffocating ago wilt and overwhelming repulse,
Life came in fast beats yet time slowed,
Surrounded by people you loved but never liked,
A moment's silence,
Away from the erratic dissonance,
Buried in debt, yet you smile,
Another lucent gesture you feign,
A craft you perfected throughout your vitality,
As the memories throb like a heartbeat in your mind,

Pain which made you temporarily blind,
The cold of the tiles,
The bee stings on your face,
The formic acid returns for a taste,
And the tears well up like a cloud about to burst,
You plough through the pain,
You keep burying it but it swells up like an overflowing stream in a storm,
Happiness remains stillborn,
You switch poisons with desire,
Enough money to inspire,
And before you walk out in your thousand-dollar pantsuit you smile the same smile;
That never reaches your eyes.
You mold yourself so perfectly that you lose your own shape,
Shattered pottery thrown in the garbage.

You Don't Belong Here

There was once a cuckoo that sang in my heart,
It played harmonies and melodies in broken parts,
It pushed out the nightingale's babies,
Spread into my ribcage like a fallen angel's melody,
An omnipresent silhouette,
I still have tapes of her songs on cassettes.
Drained me and she fluttered away,
But the cassettes were not the same,
Hunted down with Robin's arrow,
His sullying wallows,
Ruthlessly criticized,
Her spirit languidly died,
She tried to teach her beaten wings how to fly,
But it was no longer sanctioned to sail through the clear blue
Sky,
Cracked shell,
After countless wounds, it befell,
Its existence reduced to a shriveled husk,
As dawn slipped to dusk,
The nightingale weeps,
Never enough time to grieve,
Incompetence and murder
If you don't run fast enough you walk into a slaughter.

Amalgamate

Bend your chest open so I can get pick you apart,
Your finest and perfectly flawed parts
Crawl inside till I dissect and scrutinize every cell,
Willfully step on eggshells
To fall deeper inside you,
Explore every unseen hue,
Swim in your veins,
Blend into every neuron of your brain,
See my reflection in the pupils of your eyes,
Hold you captive between the cracks of your lies,
As you remember, every word I whispered in your ears,
Fill the parched well inside me with your tears,
Look at myself from your mirrors,
Feed onto your fears,
Your insecurities, your pain, your devotion,
Your love, your vigor, your validation,
Like a parasite erroneously concealed,
Never give but never fail to steal,
My touch branding your skin with my name as if pressed against heated copper
Yet you grasp onto my fingers,
Pollute you till all you can see is me,
Until I am all you feel
As I write myself on your skin,
As every inch fills with my handwriting,
Engrave myself till I become a permanent tattoo,
Till I become a part of you.

The Anarchist

Dreams soon dwindle to reality,
Decays mortality,
Time fade as clocks tick,
One no longer becomes wise but sycophantic,
One is antagonized
Yet, requisitioned to suffer with poise,
Commanded not to use your voice,
For an aristocracy is what we strive to be,
We condemn its cruelty,
But when we sin, we call it worldly.
For the fish which is bigger;
Eats the smaller,
Drunk on temporary power,
No longer the martyr.
Vigor is now debasement,
Morality is now retracement,
For this is the new world,
Where atrocities casually unfold.

The Home I Never Asked For

Take me back to my mango trees,
Fallen fruit,
Crisp leaves,
Forest of green,
The toads near the tube well,
The huge one, never afraid,
The unsaid leader,
Songs of nature,
Take me back to the peacocks,
Blue, white and muddy green,
The ray of orange falling through,
War against shielded canopy,
Somehow it always reached me,
The peacock dances till it's heart breaks;
For the peahen guards her like her peachicks,
She runs away from it like she runs away from the stray dogs;
Barking their empty threats,
Fiery logs,
Heat against my face,
Grandma's embrace,
Take me back to tree;
The one planted on her birthday,
70 and there.
Unlike her,
Take me back to the swing on it's endless branches,
One last story from your bartered home,

Take me back to the cold water,
The plunge of childhood,
Take me back to the rapid bike rides,
The bruises and broken ankles,
Take me back to the soggy fritters,
The sambar deer with their fawn.
Every summer,
Every winter,
Every spring,
Every autumn,
A child's dream,
Withered ancestry,
Her trees are gone,
So, are the peahens,
The deers,
The dogs,
What's left is the decay of debauchery;
Of avarice,
You took them away just as you took away my youth,
The last remnant of my childhood.

Red Phosphorous

Drag me like a match across the striking surface
Again, and again,
Potential yet exploited,
Give them your warmth and light
As you dwindle to cinder,
Knowing they will throw you the second you burn out;
5 seconds of fame,
But if you don't burn,
They will throw you anyway.

One Last Drink First

I'll find you at the bottom of the bottle.
History is not history if it is a generational chronicle,
Promising ourselves never to be like him,
Promises often break like silence.
Wrap me in the blanket I was born in,
Emeralds to sixpence,
Succumb to the pain you have caused,
Take me back to the friends I lost;
Remind me, they are only what friends are not meant to be.
The crystal clear water recedes,
It is only my toes sinking in the sand,
Tipped flask,
The water comes again with it's foam and infinity,
Bustling death with life writhing.
I wish I could catch a reflection of what people see in me,
The reaper's web of opacity,
Caught in it's irony,
Like one hangs from a noose,
Die than face the truth.
The Sun sets with no promise of return,
Spring is over and the tables have turned,
What have you done?
What have you become?
The world owes you nothing but a shattered ego,
Let go,

Let go,
Let go,
I won't,
I'll find you at the bottom of the bottle,
Maybe I will find myself there too.

Promise to Call When Free

I loved playing with pretty little broken things;
The kind if you were not careful with, could cut you,
Or worse,
Get you scolded,
The kind that teaches you a lesson that you refuse to learn,
But I played till my fingers bled, and the banshee screamed,
Then you came along with your undetectable sympathy,
Muddy waters in your eyes,
And hair that fell like the waterfall like I saw in Bali,
Eyes that spoke more than your parted mouth,
Skin that had the same constellation I did,
The one crooked tooth that was oddly fitted in my lower jaw just as awkward on your upper,
And I thought "Hell, not again",
Your justified kindness,
Just when I thought I did not have more to give,
You gave me just as much,
You listened, splitting me open
Just as I did the previous ones,
And every time I was in your magnetic field;
I felt just as in place as the iron fillings,
And I miss you more than I allow myself to call,
I hold on to let you go;
Cause I could not bear if I made you another pretty broken thing
But you can play with me till you get bored.

The Ringleader

I am about to lose you soon,
Born with your silver spoon.
The Sky birthed you to the dark,
Her bleeding womb a shooting star.
Mercury dripping on her fingertip,
An unfinished smile on her lips.
Real-estate future,
Anger issues borne from self-afflicted torture.
Cuff-links and small talk,
Family picture stand tall.
You had just enough girls eating at the palm of your hand,
Summer house and Malibu tan.
You had just enough boys bending over to fit you
Front and center with your everlasting youth.
Refusing to grow till you were nothing new;
You had me wanting to be you,
And the closest I could get was to be closer to you,
But do they know about what happens on the roads?
Treat yourself like a joke,
till you feel brave enough to pick up the phone.
They tore down your big top and your circus animals left you to die.
Just because you are on the tightrope doesn't mean you touched the Sky.
Narcissism kept in check by your self-doubt,
Chasing clout,

Self-destruct when you are bored,
Emotional whore,
Unconsoled,
Crying with the door closed,
Call me when you get too close,
Beg me to save you and I'll be standing at the door.
You were ocean blue,
Now you are the sick pale shade about to lose its color soon;
I know cause the same thing happened to me too.
I'm sorry:
We are nothing special no matter how desperately we want to be,
I guess I owed you the reality check and an apology.

Give in

The authors were buried;
Dead and alive.
The poets were exiled,
Rectitude was a juvenile crime.
Writers;
Weeping like widows; bleeding on paper,
Pulverizing your heart,
Sacrifice for the sake of "Art."
The angels were impaled,
There was nothing left to say,
The world was blue but the aura was gray,
The lights burst,
The stage rummaged;
Attempting to grab roses but grasping at thorns.
Tearing skin, impenetrable you thought,
Relishing nyctophilia,
Your missteps in mass media,
Beseeching ataraxia.
For poetry happens when nothing else will or can,
The final testaments of a broken man.

Fallen

When did my butterflies become moths?
They chewed holes into my hand-woven cloth.
A book cannot be a substitute for every vacuity,
I would tell you my sob story,
But it's a tale as old as time,
You could change the players, but it would still be mine,
Deftly sold,
Swallow two coins like a vending machine,
Desperate attempts to be seen,
Worked with my head down as the signs flashed before my eyes,
If only you could see the agony through mine,
I would seek solace in idols made of Midas' gold,
Then he came made of glass,
Transparent and built to never last,
He promises to set me free if I win the battle I can't win,
An eye for an eye and a queen for a king,
In the name of temporary triumph they won't give me the key,
Heavy is the head on which lies the crown,
Till the forgotten monarch is sent to the bloodhounds.
Tired of tears,
Play fair,
As they rip me apart,
Trade in a brain for a heart,

But they won't let me,
I would rather remain blindfolded for I am too scared to see.
Sleep is like a dream come true,
I know my words will be meaningless soon.

Drink Me

Am I pretty?
Will my beauty wear out with the phosphenes,
With my soulless brown eyes dripping like whiskey;
From the overflowing sink.
Loneliness, comeuppance and insecurity,
The sugary aftertaste of envy.
Parts of myself I wish I could cut free,
Stars covering my skin like a galaxy,
Lies I believe;
Happiness is temporary,
I belong to misery,
You can't leave,
You're in too deep.
Love me:
Cause I don't think you would if you knew me.
So, who do you want me to be?
Tell me?

Infringed

I haven't had a party since I was nine,
Lost all my friends because I crossed a line,
Forgive and forget when they double-crossed mine.
You know when it's one of those nights,
When you don't believe yourself when you say you are fine,
blurry eyes,
severed ties,
Winter refuses to leave and spring will perhaps come in 2025.
If I hear another speechless conversation or disdained sigh,
Why did I not just simply lie?
I was quick to learn that happiness is not something you buy;
It's a ghost to whom you say goodbye.
No manuscript and no guide,
We were taught to drown before we were taught to fly.
Demise sings her lullaby,
Fail and try,
Learn to lose and bulls-eye.

Me, Myself and I

The more you are with me the less you'll ever know,
How can someone who was never a child, grow?
No one warns you how days just get harder,
Downfall, shattered belief and you scour,
Your childhood is just the calm before the storm,
I was the experiment,
A roller-coaster's descent,
Everything you have to get wrong with to get the second one right,
The one for who you don't waste the fight,
Chasing someone else's dreams,
Sowing dormant seeds,
Losing pieces of myself,
The deeper the cut, the deeper the delve,
A scrap you know you would never get back,
You may not break but you do crack,
And even when things often don't work out,
They somehow still do,
Scratching the surface to find something to hold onto,
You take the first thing that comes your way,
You pray it stays,
Shame, remorse, disgust
Deeply bonds than the friends you once trusted,
Maybe I have been choosing the wrong people,
Never forgive and never show yourself as feeble,
But I have always been the wrong person every time,

Too boring, too quick to cross the line,
I'm sick of being the second favorite,
Desperate to hear it,
Second choice,
The muted voice,
Second best,
And soon you settle for less,
Pity my reflection,
Fatal attraction,
Twisted flesh,
Flawed, reckless and wrecked,
And you trade your heart in for a dream you will never achieve,
Never ready but always wanting to leave,
And you hate yourself for never being good enough,
Tough love,
And you sleep with the blanket of humiliation every night,
Pray for dreamless sleep and clutch it tight,
Drown,
Be found.

Woman

As dawn manifested itself in the mauve Sky,
A beautiful baby girl covered in blood bore her first cry,
She didn't even get a chance to look into her mother's eyes,
As they poured sand down her throat while she writhed for life.

As the Sun reached its pinnacle,
A girl went to school pedaling on her bicycle,
She noticed a black car following her,
Soon as she turned around the secluded corner,
In less than a split second, she felt a jolt;
Hands tied, cold hand on her mouth, eyes blindfolded,
Not older than fifteen,
Never to be seen.

The Sun returned to its horizon in frigid winter,
The January chill hard to bear,
It was a perfectly normal day,
She had no idea what awaited,
She stepped inside her house,
Soon to be found on the floor,
Raped and murdered,
Front page of the newspaper,
As her parents seek justice against his crimes,
He goes on living a perfectly mundane life.

The Moonlight shone
giving her face a luminous glow,
head against the window,
Just as they grabbed her and pushed her against the floor,
And did indefinable things to her behind the bus's door.
How could someone do something this vile?
Six men and one just a juvenile.
How she must have screamed?
How she must have wept?
Her misery, her pain,
How in those few moments, everything changed,
Soon to be found on the corner of some street,
Succumbed to her injuries.

The stars twinkled as the tiny girl;
In the plastic bag giggled.
Found a less than a week later;
In the corner of a trash can as vermin ran over her,
Skin smeared with mud,
Hands covered in cuts and her fingertips coated in dry blood,
Face white as a sheet,
Rotting debris covering her feet,
Thrown away, exiled,
How could someone do this to their own child?

The red rooftops glistened in the Moonlight,
As the clock struck midnight.
The million-dollar house in a high society province;
Where crimes partook beyond our imagination,

Just as voices began to raise,
He slapped her across the face,
Dragging her to a dark room as he grabbed her hair,
Their children standing frozen with fear,
He locked the door decorating her body with bruises,
As she endured these atrocious skirmishes,
Soon two men in black held her insentient cadaver,
Give the power and pay the price forever.

You are either a slut or a prude,
A people pleaser or rude,
A bitch if you establish boundaries,
Sit still and look pretty,
Feminism is just women being dramatic,
A man being cruel is pragmatic,
A woman being strategic
Is manipulative,
A household is derailed by her career
Reduced to a whisper,
It's lonely at the top but I hear it's one hell of a view,
They will hate you no matter what you do,
Play for your team,
Fight for what you believe.

Moonlight Swims

It scared me the first time;
How different the world looked when it wasn't in black and white,
When it was not on fire.
Heavenly torture reserved for liars,
When it isn't on fast forward and every instant is in slow-motion,
No longer tormented by my own shadows.
The ephemeral silence,
The sedation of the scathing, discontented, resentful voice in my head,
The unpolluted void.
My sanity swiped through detoured Polaroids,
Trivial faces,
Unidentified names.
The provisional exhilaration from the needless baggage,
Friends I could save but didn't;
Now lost in caged salients.
Phantoms which kept me up at night,
Now merely unfamiliar faces bleached by the Moonlight.
The ground below my feet slipping,
The stars in the dark falling,
I wanted to call someone,
But I didn't want to hear anything reasonable at all,
Mesmerized by this exorbitant feeling,
This synthetic fleeting feeling.

Tomorrow was Worse

The tube light flickers,
Sunday mania and eyes closed in rapture,
Every time my dreams shatter,
I make new ones from the broken pieces,
My eyes hurt, and my back hunches,
Hiding myself in me,
The pieces keep getting smaller,
The puzzle harder,
People die, friends escape,
Unexplored insecurity take shape.
T.V don't leave me,
Keep me away from reality,
Fall back into 'Modern Family';
Till we numb enough to fall into a dreamless sleep.
The tube light bursts,
How could tomorrow possibly be worse?

Ripple Drip

My past haunts my present for it folds into my future,
My heart races against time as the neurons in my brain rupture,
Constructing more detrimental maps,
Mending to only relapse.

The gelid of the marble slab on which I rest my knuckles,
My bones scraping against each other tasting metal,
The fogginess of the mirror,
My blood rushing into my brain as liquor.

The raspy breath in the steam of the scalding rain,
The hidden bliss of the somatic ache
Scouring to perfection,
The burning red of the tender flesh,
I gather the intrepidity to meet my own gaze,
In the black hole of pupils flash the recollections of the dog days,
Stare into his eyes sewn onto my face like buttons,
The alternative for his penance.

I reminiscence the shame of exile,
Those memories become perpetual when they should be senile,
The dread, the contempt, the suppressed anger,
Soon to erupt as I run out of paper.

Lycanthropy

The iris pollutes the pupil,
Sealing the darkness' nuptial,
A red Moon, a pit in hell,
Ciphered verses of the bible,
Muffled cries and a hopeless ritual,
Fingers grow backwards
To form twisted tapered talons,
Your backbends, and the skin wrinkles and scales
Every tendon in your body snaps,
Every bone breaks to create a new map,
Fangs tearing out of your gums as if a snakes
Icicles stemming from your bronchioles piercing through your lungs,
Your heart recklessly aging, no longer young,
The pristine red rivers now run venom,
The final verse now sung,
Your once child-like piety now an eyesore,
This curse is no longer folklore,
Shelled in your body,
Your pallid beauty.

Battlegrounds

I believe I was born with a bullet inside my body,
A silver shard
Which tore my empty vessel apart,
Now a part of my identity.
The conical structure was present long before I was begotten,
A fervid metal wrapped around by my muscles,
Broken bones, snapped tendons and self-healed aneurysms,
It corrodes and rots with time, bestrewing its venom,
The malefic curse reserved a particular fondness for my brain,
And if it was silent enough, I could hear the gunshots,
It is devised to do as much damage as it can before it dissolves,
When dark enough, I could see its coruscate,
It ensures it tears through every neuron,
But it stays away from the hippocampus,
It knows that blissful damage will make its detrimental purpose,
It knows its sempiternal puissant,
It rends till it finally dissolves,
Acidifies my ichor,
with nothing to reach for.

Blueprint

Your murals daubed across my chapels,
Polishing my shovels,
Burying you in a bottomless pit of my heart,
Locking you in a treasure chest as priceless art,
Reminiscing the curve of your lip,
The lines on your fingers' tip,
The almost invisible hook of your nose,
Your fluorescent glow,
Pessimal,
Your eyes drenched in burnt caramel,
Every strand of muscle in your body,
Your portraits spread across my gallery,
Every vibrant color,
Vandalizing my mind as if a tumor,
Holding onto every detail, I emanated from rumors,
Stolen photos,
Internet glamor,
Every fragment as I glanced at your silhouette from the window,
Who were you?
I believe I just have to piece the clues.

Why does pain have to have purpose?

The Sky is purple today,
I am thinking of all the lessons I could have learned without the pain
But then they wouldn't be worth remembering,
Burning,
Isn't it imprisoning?

The Half-Broken Heart Necklace

One and one makes a broken heart,
Bring up the guard,
My misery is a game not an art,
Forgotten moments and birthday cards torn apart,
Down goes the house of cards
But I will rebuild,
Time holds my hand as we fail to stay still:
"Chill",
So many things left unsaid,
I stayed calm and watched as you climbed onto your deathbed,
Selfish, repulsive and ugly,
Said you were too "Busy",
My win did not have to be your loss,
Or the cause
Of your vagary,
You lost a friend but sure did win my pity,
A drama-addicted harlequin,
I find your state more rueful than despicable,
Thereby, I leave you to dethrone yourself,
A twin bound to annihilate herself,
Everything revolved around her fallen kingdom,
An exhausted justification but the perfect victim,
You will never be happy
Because you simply don't deserve to be,
Everyone who truly loves you will see you

For the real you,
I bolted because that would be the boldest thing I could do,
Never forgive and never forget,
Taking myself back to all the wrong things you said,
You look different now,
You feel different, how?
A poem written dedicated to you I promised,
Only under other circumstances I wish,
Fake friends fail in adversity;
That's the difference between you and me.

You Have 0 Messages

I hate Instagram:
Not because of the same pathetic, "It's too distracting" reason
But cause every single time I swipe;
Up,
Right,
Down,
Left,
I waste a second I could have spent killing myself,
Seconds turn to hours
And I would look at my empty seat and my unfinished work,
Feel remorse,
Beyond duty,
Alone,
Secluded in my room, pretending it's by choice,
Feel more tragic
As I see the pretty girls
Falling for pretty lies,
I tell myself they will soon be nothing but trophy wives,
Falling for men I see as steroid-riddled, testosterone-fueled idiots,
Easy,
Genuine sympathy,
No matter how desperately I crave superiority;
I cannot wish more than to be a part of them,

Seek consolation in the same false sense of security and groupism,
Believe I am a part of something bigger than myself,
Think they would always stand by me
But they didn't
And you know that,
Attend the concerts I shouldn't have missed,
Come back starved of attention,
And laugh for no reason,
The parties they talk about,
The friends who should have been,
The makeup you never had time to buy,
The clothes that never fit right on your skin but is like their second,
The music that never matches your heartbeat as it does theirs,
Poses which make you look desperate,
Smiles which seem too ingenuine,
The fourth wheel,
The shouldn't have been,
The one who regrets coming
But attends for the sake of showing up
Ends up having a better time than rotting away
And thinks,
Thinks for a second,
Huh
Isn't this easy,
Not wonderful,
But so easy,
The stars miss the Sun,

And as I see outside into the abyss;
Beyond the curtains that should be closed,
I just spent two hours on the phone,
Maybe I am my own worst enemy,
Damn it
I have a project due at 11:59.

The Child Born With A Broken Heart

Some of us are born with broken wings,
Broken hearts and broken dreams,
A hammer and sickle in hand,
A crypt to dig,
Promise of the pot of gold at the end of the rainbow,
A hope to make us whole.

The Mahogany Shelf With Bluebirds And Cherries

I want enough books to fill up a home;
One for every story I should have told,
- Every party I did not attend but wanted to because I had no one I wanted to talk to,
- A friend I could have made if I went anyway,
- Cities I would have hopped a train to,
- Dresses I wanted twirl into,
- Love someone I never knew,
- Admire art I don't care about in the Louvre
- Laugh till it echoes in my chest telling me it's real,
- Crimes I almost would have got caught committing,
- Taste wine for the first time in Italy,
- Falling out of caravans, almost not fitting,
- Strangers with whom I would not have pretend to be someone else,
- Posted about me for me rather than just scroll,
- An apology I owed,
- Inspire beyond woe,

I want to be liked despite my flaws like the characters
Make mistakes which remain confined to paper,
Reckless,
Careless,
Feel everything and turn to the next page,
Comfort in existence,
Know my worth is being documented,
Even if it means nothing,

It's some place on a shelf somewhere,
Tenderly in someone's hands,
The bucket list for my uncarried out plans,
I realize I have more bookmarks than books,
I have no one to blame but myself
Because no one has been crueler to me
Than me.

Make Mistakes But Don't Repeat Them

Sometimes you have to lose sight to gain perspective,
But now I am blind.

Dealer

Nights feels different,
Tales partook in warm silence,
Reality fades,
Secrets exchanged,
My mind feels numb,
I reminisce joy seldom,
High on induced serotonin,
Overdosed on desolation,
You blankly stare at door knobs, notebooks and windows,
Forbidden sustenance,
And even as you are half asleep
You can see,
Not in glimpses,
Not in edited scenes from movies
But see,
Actually see,
Through the cracks and the defects,
Through the false hopes,
Defeated heroes,
Twisted stories and special effects,
The world seems perfect,
Broken but perfect.

Pride

Resisting my drapetomania,
My mid-morning mania,
This copious urge to surrender;
Rummaged and murdered
By emphatic predators,
Expectancies and aspirations;
Stampeding my inspirations,
I waved the white flag,
Aggravated by my setbacks,
Fail and forced to try,
I'm so tired,
My aeipathy disintegrated,
Tired of my failures,
My futile endeavors,
I wanted to burn my paper plans,
The flames searing my hands
Yet I held on like a tenacious infant,
Desperate to ascertain something insignificant,
I let myself be ruined by relentless defeat,
My heart is wilting to concrete.

Puppet

Acouasm making my ears bleed

Yet, the briny tang on the tip of my tongue was sweet,

My soul ardent

Yet, benumbed,

Razbliuto burned my heart like acid,

Madness left my mind avid,

Nothing was ever poetic,

I altered prosaic to magic,

Authenticity from plastic

Made the darkness hypnotic,

The burst of color when the world was nothing but sardonic,

Yet, all I was seen was as problematic,

Mundane, tedious, psychotic,

Satirized for my pursuits, my aspirations,

Bleeding out from my lacerations,

Deep cuts

Crucified by the blue bloods,

The other dragged the corpse of the sacrificed,

Wretched, vulnerable, demonized,

When all I did was try to survive,

Make it out of this crippling fever alive,

That part of me still roams around the dim-lit streets

Of my uncertifiable mind,

In shackles looking for a haven to hide,

As I lay with the lamp on the bedside:

My skin a sick blue,
My cracked lips sewed,
Skin under dried blood,
The water rushed in from the flash flood,
I sat there with a laptop on my lap
Clicking every testament of mine on a keypad,
As the water choked me,
I drowned in my melancholy.

Break Me or I Will Break You

Your rutilant glow in the dim lights,
Promise shone in your callow eyes,
Beautiful lies,
As you listened patiently like a compliant child,,
Mystified,
As you twinkled your innocent smile,
Your dark hair, which I stroked my hands through,
Burying my face in you,
As I inhaled your perfume
Wrapped in each other,
Silence, dysfunction and careless laughter,
I pressed your forehead against mine,
The moreen curtains shadowed the Sunlight,
There was a blank space
In my heart where I waited
For all those years,
You arrived like a beacon of color,
Wiping away the tears,
Holding my hand as you buoyantly help me face my fears,
And I walked through the discounted fire,
Clasping onto me like a treasured sapphire,
The world unwound into madness as I built my fortress around you;
Laying the bricks until my hands bruised blue,
It was the kind of devotion for which people desired,
wandered for, desperately looked

But found it forced in movies, fairy tales, and books,
Yet I uncovered ways to abuse it,
Defied the fundamental postulates,
Walked out the door when the heat was too much to take,
Never accepted my mistakes,
Pointed fingers for I never took the blame,
Unnecessary games,
Until your smile was barely a show of teeth,
The scars seethed,
Silly fights which we would joke about soon turned to unmet gazes and screams,
Threatening each other to leave,
Your eyes couldn't even look at me
Until all we did was sit in lamentable speechlessness,
For the bud had turned venomous,
For every word we spoke to each other was filled with bitterness,
Hopelessness rendered me powerless,
As I watched you with your bags packed;
You walked out the blue door, not looking back,
While I sank on the floor with my heart collapsed,
With my crumpled fortress, bleak memories, our perished pacts.

Monday

I built myself, as a child assembles blocks
Only for the playground bully to break them down,
A flash of pain across your cheek and a twisted ankle,
Hidden skeletons in the cradle,
They expect you to sit silent,
Blood-curdling screams and forgiven violence,
Bear the evermore hollowing pain;
A smile plastered on your face
To be crucified for acting on survival but not what you are told,
Scheming oaths and emotional vitriol,
A never escaping spiral,
A gold-plated victim card and a corroded muzzle,
Playing 'Beautiful Stranger' on the broken guitar,
I wonder if anyone will bear with me my fractured bones and bleeding scars,
But what do you want me to do with all this wasted time,
Lowest of lows and highest of highs,
Dismay and betting dollars to dimes,
A newfound core memory,
An epilogue of my journey on this beggary,
Sometimes running away is the boldest thing you can do,
Take a deep breath and face the truth,
Don't discount because you have to,
Let the Sun enwrap you just as effortlessly as the deep ocean blues.

They Call Me Cruel

I think women are born into families where there is not enough space for them,
And they are sold into families which have no space for an equal.

Will you be there for the bedtime story

Fade;
Like you were never there,
I would sleep scared
Of nightmares which were more real,
I would wait for the stories of Ben, the red dragon,
The wizard in the cave, his house by the lake and his uptight mum,
How he would lose the tennis match to his adversary?
You forgot to tell me there were two enemies,
The ambushing visits of his mother,
The complaints, the mess and the unnecessary laundry, but you never spoke of his father,
Maybe I don't remember,
The wicked sorceress and her twisting spells,
Across the seven seas and bad motels,
His stolen vegetables from the garden which he grew,
The burrowed rat and the broom which flew,
The hilltop and the camping trip,
The kidnapped princess saved by valiant knightship,
The loch ness monster in the lake,
Trade words for pain,
Eight months went by without the barter,
The dragon with the golden scales was a cover,
Everything you never gave me:
False sense of security,
A childhood of false affirmation,

Every betrayal a harder lesson,
Every broken lock you didn't repair,
Every lie you swore by,
Every broken bottle seal,
I bury everything but the stories,
You have been dead since a decade,
Yet you always chose when to fade,
Leaving a blemish of scarlet returning for a bitter taste,
Imprinted like a stain,
You still leave but never the despair.

Run

At 15 we were all given an ultimatum,
Stuttering heartbeats ensnared in the same asylum,
The gods told us to reap the future or the past;
Lose ourselves to time that wouldn't last,
Under the shadow of the grim reaper,
Squandered away to fear,
Time was a ripping seam between life and death;
Reminding us of every wasted breathe,
I refuse to die here,
Collapsing societies,
Paralyzing anxiety,
I'll hold on,
I'll hold on to these undeluded memories.

I feel stuck in between
Yet driven to extremes,
My throat swelling with accountability,
My heart pumping through clots of eccentricity.

The dizzying spell of ecstasy
Forced beliefs in fallacy;
Entertainment purposes only.

The disquieting respite I encountered in the fissures of my lies;
For not all caterpillars come out to be beautiful butterflies.

I'll hold on believing it would set me free;
I refuse to forfeit this stampede.

The Door is Wide Open

You could lay me as gently as you want in my bed,
But know that I will not rest,
Not till I can sense the rhythm of your breathe,
Of a language that can only be felt,
You dropped my hand just as you dropped my heart,
They always told us not to shoot bullets in a house of glass,
sunlight burned through the shards,
The Jack of spades loses all for the sake of the queen of hearts,
Thinking it to be better to be the master of none than some,
Our abandoned mansion caught fire,
Do not mistake this for an accident but a crossfire.

Ice Sliding down my back

Stay,
The same ,
Because I don't have what it takes to grow up to have you wither away,
A name which hurts to even overhear in the hallway,
I cut my hand polishing your shovels,
We dug a grave to win the race to the center of the earth,
Blunt force trauma and blackout,
Wake up to realize that it is the deathbed,
You have made for yourself,
My nails are chipped,
Sand solidified between the lines of my hand,
In too deep to get out,
The only way we know is down,
I come out the other end ,
Only to realize it did not have to be this hard to begin with.

Alone and Lonely

I find myself abandoned
In delight of puerile laughter and glum of abounding prisons;
Between gardens of manic and sanity,
Childish games of divinity,
Despite having the ability to walk out free;
Bound to slavery,
Unwilling misery,
I find myself back to where I began when these paradoxes lose their novelty.

I fear closing my eyes,
The voices ancillaries to my insanity,
As I hold my breath straining to discern reality,
My mind serving as my penitentiary.

My afflictions grow more indocile,
My skin less versatile,
I yearn to be carried away by the tide,
A sign of better times,
As I dip my head in the cool liquid
And feel the warm orange on my eyelids.

I dream of restful sleep,
Blurry blues as I dives into the deep,
The sweet derange of passion,
The feverish frenzy of devotion.

I long for unabridged silence,
Controlled madness,
Indubitable credence,
Balance.

The Girl with The Sun Tattoo

I always thought she would be rough
But her skin was the softest I had ever touched:
Like milk in which honey from her eyes dripped,
I wish
I could sip it all up,
You and I are cut from the same cloth,
Drawn to the same flame like moths,
The line parting her lips a bridge,
The kind you cross
And burn down to forgive your sins,
My thumb traced down the tip of her chin,
The nape of her neck,
The heart of her chest,
And hooked on to her bellybutton
I placed my ear against her,
And I heard not her heartbeat but a forest;
Another world,
Chittering squirrels,
Cheshire cats with question marked tails,
Cicadas,
Falling pink guava,
The whistling trees,

A stream
With its silverfish and stories,

Then there was me,

I pulled back when I heard the creak
Of the bridge,
A sound I knew all too well,
Some rebuild,
Force us to confront what we don't want to acknowledge,
I thought this time I would be special.

Participation Trophy

I was the participation trophy but never the prize,
Poorly made tainted alloy,
Neglected,
Rusting in the bottom of your drawer,
The kind you put away
And now look at every morning in admiration,
Budding disappoinment,
You don't lift me up without feeling the burden of your own failure,
Your time gone to waste,
Hard work gone in vain.

Smile for the Camera

I stand nevertheless trapped like a magician caged dove,
The fervent crowd anticipating my marvel hoax,
A mere vestige of a dullard bloke,
My voodoo on the clueless crowd,
When I would rather fly among the clouds ,
I sometimes think
Would it silence the beast
This pent up anger,
Drained by this numbness,
Thirst that knows no end,
Satiated by this abandonment,
Dragging down whoever is closest,
If I knew myself I would know who to miss,
Drifting away,
Tell me the point of staying,
Center stage starlet,
Wave the white flag of your forfeit,
Angels sing the final chorus,
The fluorescent lights,
Stinging my eyes,
Every step seems heavier,
Every breath feels as though my lungs are penetrating me with spears,
The corridors were narrowing,
The classrooms were suffocating,
I felt sick to my very gut,

Surgeon lights brightening the blood,
The shriveled rosebud,
My sentiments had died,
Forgotten principles to live by,
Buried somewhere I can't find,
Whispers turned to screams,
incomplete crime scene,
The jury was corrupt,
The verdict was abrupt,
The convict set free,
The evidence was foreseen,
The innocent was exiled,
Never to be the shine to your Moonlight.

Predictable

Dusk sets a newfangled aurora,
Irreversible karma,
But dawn is worse
For another day passes,
And an uncontaminated origin is brought to life,
You shall be revived
Only to poison this new beginning,
Only to abuse your blessing,
I ruin things on purpose and complain about how things could have been,
Maybe people like me can never indeed be happy,
Your choices feel like a burden;
Wishing to abandon.

Captive

My doleful shadows:
Ruthless, tenacious, spiteful, shallow,
Your radiant Sunshine:
Charming, steady, sensible, polite,
My impetuous gambles
Leaving perfection in shambles,
Your clever gambits
Veneering the depravity of my secrets
As I aver my unconvincing justifications,
Clouding my conscience,
Imploring me to do the right thing,
Your calming consolations in the downcast mornings,
My fatuity fueled by my flummadiddle,
Our fallen capitol:
Cynical and quixotic,
Which poison to pick,
You deserved more
But I couldn't bring myself to let you go,
Your kindness,
Your controlled madness
Mendacious to my callous,
Fervid to my convoluted love,
Reigning these turbulent seas,
Too familiar to leave

Your warmth over me,
Power to be lost soon;
Lying next to each other, expecting some miraculous breakthrough.

Void

The higher the pedestal;
Your downfall will be only a grander the spectacle,
Pink champagne glasses clinking at your funeral,
Your name at their disposal,
At war with yourself in a losing battle,
Fighting against the inevitable,
Holding onto what isn't mine,
You dissolve into the sands of time,
Blazing Sunshine,
Hope no longer a ray of light,
Persevering on droplets in your flask,
Foes unmasked,
The droplet evaporates before it touches your tongue,
Triumph does not prevail as long as defeat does,
The shards of my ruinate dreams punctured my lungs through,
The bruises fade but never the scars,
Bury me with my ambition in the broken dream's graveyard,
I know my way up,
I don't need a pat on the back or a consoling hug,
The foretelling or the "concern", they expressed,
They forget this is not the first time I've risen from the dead.

Name

I wish people were as intrigued by me as they are by my name;
At times I think me and my name are separate entities,
My name is not fit for another person crossing the street
Like me,
Monotony hidden under a false identity.

Bedside Tea

I no longer slept in the corner of my bed where I fell off,
But right in the middle with my back against yours ,
Feel the rise and fall,
Of your body and warmth ,
misery is better company than most people can be ,
Lurking third wheel,
Waiting for you to let down your shield,
Our house could be on fire but all you would do is look at me,
I no longer play to win but have all my cards on the table,
No more gambles,
I 'll tell you what I have never told anyone from the start,
Of how I burned, crashed and fell apart.what I want.

Bitten Back Words

Wrenching into each other;
We fell in love in colours
Blue, pink, ebony and purple,
Melting into the other,
Corroding and blending,
Twisting into the things we never believed in,
Until another could never touch even an inch,
Bitter tincture,
Cured but never the same,
Comforted knowing we were stuck on the thin line we cross to claim,
Even when we closed our eyes apart from another;
We could feel the cord which tied the other,
The chaos and suffering which bound us,
The pain we relished in turning us to dust,
But we knew it was impossible to love someone
If you knew them well enough.

Maps

When the Sun and Moon share the Sky,
As it turns pink,
Blushing,
Over the black sea,
And the stars and clouds join hands,
Will you come,
With the same liberty as that photo you posted in front of the Pacific Ocean;
Joint in hand, high on pride,
Can you put me out of misery like it?
Do you wish the memories evaporated just as the smoke did
Or am I the inebriety which sticks to your lungs?
You can't cough me up,
As the Sun cascades into the darkness of infinity,
Pink turns to angry orange,
They depart,
Uncertain,
For all great loves must come to an end,
Do you think about me like I think about you,
While you thrive somewhere
At the edge of the world?
In club heaven, with its forgotten past and blinding lights
Or do they not let you enter because only I could be your paradise,
Do you still watch Sunsets
And think about that moment we lost;

When we forgot we were merely mortals,
Are you still friends with the people who warned you about me?
Are you beginning to see through me like they did
Or am I the one you can't bring yourself to hate?
Do you still dress like a twelve-year old kid?
Brown cargo shorts, the t-shirt between red and maroon, illuminating Sunshine
Reflecting in your eyes,
Glistening over your hair,
Bouncing off your skin,
Did you finally find the beach where the Sun and the Moon met
Or are you still blue,
Are you still searching
Like I am?
Stuck in this big city with its small minds,
While you are someplace where I wish I were with you.

The Better Whole But I Gave You My Half

You taste like blood on a bitten tongue;
With your salty metallic agony,
Humbling pride,
Silencing empathy,
Undertones of superiority;
Not said
But sensed,
I role you at the back of my tongue;
Swallow you whole,
You can still find him if you reach for the back of my throat,
Would you stay in one place
Or jump from one cobblestone to another?
Burning everything to the ground
Like you always do
And begin building on the ashes like they never existed,
Sometimes I wonder if you would burn me too,
But your eyes say otherwise
With their twinkling demise,
One might call them mundane
But if you look carefully enough, you can see the whole world in them,
Your swimmer's body
Gliding into me,
Misery loves company

And I wonder if I climb on top of you,
Will I ever be equal,
Not in your eyes
But mine?
But I come
From places
You would call hell,
I don't kiss and tell.

Blackthorn Flowers

The subtle sensation of monachopsis follows you like a dreary cloud,
People asphyxiate me,
Brandishing frivol credentials yet sufficed with vanity,
They were as hollow as the bottles that they drain,
The medical cabinets that they raid,
Melancholy felt enervating;
Pitifully everlasting,
Anxiety was like a ticking time bomb,
Angel's sacred psalm,
Raw, blinding fury,
I was incensed by myself,
My moonstruck heart ate itself ,
Piece by piece,
Savoring the menace,
Strayed,
Pulverizing your forte,
It made me concede how alone I was,
Midnight and pointless conversations
With people who left me
Calmed my explosions,
And I found fragments of serenity
In veracity.

Letter

Hi
I haven't seen you since a while,
I don't know why;
Actually, that was a lie,
You switched sides,
I'm too scared to ask you,
Altered versions of the truth,
I made you immortal
Only for you to labeled me as the problem,
I overheard;
Ear to the door,
Debased coward
And a perfidious traitor,
I can't really say who's who,
I always prided myself on not losing
Battles and things,
So I tell myself I sacrificed it,
They aren't synonyms,
Trusting lies,
Faithful denial,
I asked the magic eight ball why people hate me,
I threw it before it could tell me,
Confrontation is often worse,
Might as well share a shrug in the corridor.

Come Back nanu, "I Owe You"

I will never call your name to have you turn around to my voice,
Tutti frutti ice cream with you to complete the summer,
Small talk and boasting about me to your pals,
Passed on duties to fulfill,
No more flash of orange and white kurta in the park;
Your mark,
Hands behind your back and head held high,
Humble yet dignified,
Bitter yet true,
Remembered but gone too soon,
You left a hole in my heart,
Come back,
Teach me to fix it before it breaks in half,
Come back and tell me all the stories you never told,
All the lessons to fold,
All the advice I need;
We are lost without your lead,
Map of your memories,
It's not enough to go on without holding your hand;
Take me back to the only home I ever had,
Sun-kissed like a farmer,
Suit made of armor,
Clear, hazy eyes;
Ear-to-ear smile,
A recollection to find,

Cherished sign of times,
Never knew the power of what was mine,
A red blemish,
Magical foresight and infinite knowledge,
Red face and cane chairs,
Sunlight, swings, and fritters,
I see old men with their turbans and collared shirts,
Hope they would turn and I see your face;
I see wandering souls on the street and not you,
I go to sleep wishing to see you,
Glimpses are enough
To know you are fine,
I put flowers in front of your photo,
The winter your vegetable garden didn't grow,
Catching the tiny toads,
Please don't leave us alone,
I'll meet you at the terminal of heathrow airport.

www.ingramcontent.com/pod-product-compliance
Lightning Source LLC
LaVergne TN
LVHW041627070526
838199LV00052B/3274